NAMES
POEMS

ALSO BY MARILYN HACKER

MARILYN HACKER

NAMES

POEMS

W. W. NORTON & COMPANY

New York · London

For information about permission to reproduce selections from
this book, write to Permissions, W. W. Norton & Company, Inc.,
500 Fifth Avenue, New York, NY 10110

For information about special sales for bulk purchases,
please contact W. W. Norton Special Sales at
specialsales@wwnorton.com or 800-233-4830

Manufacturing by Courier Westford
Book design by Charlotte Staub
Production manager: Anna Oler

Library of Congress Cataloging-in-Publication Data

Hacker, Marilyn, 1942–
Names : poems / Marilyn Hacker.—1st ed.
p. cm.
ISBN 978-0-393-07218-1
I. Title.
PS 3558.A28N36 2010
811'.54—dc22   2009032422

W. W. Norton & Company, Inc.
500 Fifth Avenue, New York, N.Y. 10110
www.wwnorton.com

W. W. Norton & Company Ltd.
Castle House, 75/76 Wells Street, London W1T 3QT

1 2 3 5 6 6 7 8 9 0

CONTENTS

AN OCEAN BETWEEN US

NAMES

BLASONS

GRATEFUL ACKNOWLEDGMENT is given to the editors of the publications in which many of these poems first appeared: *Asheville Poetry Review*; *Bat City Review*; *Bayou*; *Bloom*; *Commonweal*; *The Gay and Lesbian Review*; *The Kenyon Review*; *Magma*; *The Manhattan Review*; *The Massachusetts Review*; *Modern Poetry in Translation*; *The New England Review*; *New Letters*; *Nightsun*; *Pleiades*; *PN Review*; *Poetry Daily*; *Poetry International*; *Poetry London*; *Poetry Northwest*; *Poetry Review*; *Prairie Schooner*; *The Progressive*; *Upstairs at Duroc*; *upstreet*; *The Virginia Quarterly Review*; *The Walrus*; *Water-Stone Review*; *The Yale Review*

"Be mindful of names. They'll etch themselves . . ." was first published in *The New Yorker*.

"Glose: Storm" appeared in the *Pushcart Prize XXX: Best of the Small Presses*, Pushcart Press, 2006.

"For Kateb Yacine" appeared in *The Best American Poetry 2005,* edited by Paul Muldoon and David Lehman, Scribner.

"Ghazal: Waiting" appeared in *Poetry Daily Essentials, 2007,* edited by Diane Boller and Don Selby, Sourcebooks.

"O Caravels" by Guy Goffette appeared in *Charlestown Blues,* poems by Guy Goffette, translated by Marilyn Hacker, University of Chicago Press, 2007.

Section XLVII from "The Year of the Dragon" by Emmanuel Moses appeared in *Last News of Mr. Nobody,* poems by Emmanuel Moses, translated by Marilyn Hacker and others, Other Press, 2005.

The excerpt from "Nettles" by Vénus Khoury-Ghata appeared in *Nettles,* poems by Vénus Khoury-Ghata, translated by Marilyn Hacker, The Graywolf Press, 2008.

"Storm" by Claire Malroux appeared in *Birds and Bison,* poems by Claire Malroux, translated by Marilyn Hacker, Sheep Meadow Press, 2004.

The excerpt from "Willow" by Anna Akhmatova, translated by Judith Hemschemeyer, appeared in *The Complete Poems of Anna Akhmatova,* Zephyr Press, 1997.

LAUDS

LAUDS

Ghazal: In Summer

For Mimi Khalvati

The air thickens, already more than half in summer.
At the corner café, girls in T-shirts laugh in summer.

The city streets, crowded with possibility
under spring rain, thin out, don't promise enough in
      summer.

That urge to write one's life instead of living it
makes sentences slip limply off-the-cuff in summer.

Slipped in a drawer under an expired passport,
curly-head in an orchard smiles for a photograph in summer.

Going downstairs early for bread: two winos snore on the
      landing,
"Can't they make do with sleeping in the rough in summer?"

Hard-case on the street, teacher out of class both harbor
a lowgrade fever and productive cough in summer.

Espresso winter, springtime of Juliénas:
black tea with honey's what I'll quaff in summer.

Despite my wall of books and Bach's geometries,
some scent wafts from the street to call my bluff in summer.

Not in a tank but a golf cart rides the oligarch:
however, he does not dismiss his staff in summer.

Let them not, in Maryam's name or Marilyn's,
blot any cindered city off a graph in summer.

Lauds

Inhabit daylight, unfurl where it's found
filtering through the curtain, where there is
a cup circled with steatopygous
peaches floating on white porcelain.
Given, the tintinnabulation in
the ears at dusk will usefully pipe down
behind some music, street-noise smorgasbord,
hiss of a loss, of what's not possible
any longer, that's a shell clamped shut
on an unpromising fragment of grit
although a nacreous mother-of-pearl
sky is contained within. A dozen plump
oysters of hours, plate of a winter day
embossed with cloudy gilt chinoiserie.
The hours are hung with clouds, not flags,
epiphanous, ephemeral. Light drags
down, lingers more briefly, fades and dims
to indoor warmth, domestic solstice hymns.

Praise even the tea-stained quadrilled paper, praise
the notebook which descended three decades
untouched, with yellowed charts of Latin verbs,
genealogies, datelines of empires,
kings and academicians being crowned
on pages years of claustral air had browned.
I opt for its utility and fill
its pages in a language it was not
intended for, but it is innocent
of opinions, unless I need some tense
of *laudare* or an approximate

date for the archetypal Trojan War.
Now, maculated by some matinal
buttered bread, or coffee, while it rained
outside, its gesture is a curve, embrace
of what's within the arc, time within place.

Le Sancerre: July

Your morning guts slowed down by Migralgine,
you caffeinate into a present tense
where nothing makes as much of a difference
as sunlight on the fanned spectrum of green
post-solstice foliage overflowing the square
—japonica, mimosa, *marronnier.*
Two small black girls on bikes wobble and sway
toward balance on the shaded sidewalk where
secular newlyweds leave the Mairie.
Disaster is inexorable somewhere:
a timed device; treads of a bulldozer,
no more contained by meter than by free
salsa concerts, miscegenation in July
or dependable black coffee at Le Sancerre.

Ghazal: Across the Street

Three cops—what are they waiting for across the street?
I'd make some quip, but you're not with me, or across the
     street.

Sedentary traveler, facing my window
blinds rise on provinces I still explore across the street.

Who'll move into the newly renovated four-room
flat (opposite mine) on the fourth floor across the street?

I bought *Le Monde* late afternoons at the newsstand
replaced by one more pricey menswear store across the
     street.

I still knot a scarf to stand in the bakery line
—you teased me, for caring what I wore across the street.

Fat drops fall. Shoppers huddle under the awning
till the bus comes. It starts to pour across the street.

I write "you," shorthand for one more absence.
A motorcycle revs up with a roar across the street.

The bus heads eastward with its sodden passengers
out of my vision like a metaphor across the street.

Now the cops—two boys, one girl, not thirty—
seem less inquisitive than jocular across the street.

The rain has stopped as quickly as it started
but there's no news-fix anymore across the street.

If they imagine women forget dead babies
in those countries, they don't imagine war across the street.

A window opens like a book on evening,
Light silvers grillwork on a door across the street.

Pollution gives the sky to feral pigeons.
They coo over more territory than before across the street.

Above the frieze of chimneys, antennas and window gables,
swallows in V-formation used to soar across the street.

Glose

Staying put provides the solidest
comfort as daylight diminishes at four:
the street becomes, again, a palimpsest
of hours, days, months and years that came before
and what is better was, and what is best
will be its distillation. In the pause
when blinds are drawn, when tea is brewed, when fast-
falling evening makes lamplight seem more
private and privileged, I can be still because
a child, I knew how sweet departure was

and planned, extravagantly, voyages,
encounters, divagations, chronicles
of travel, unpronounced truths, bright lies.
Imagined stonework of façades, and smells
not of tinned soup or ink. Gratuitous
enormities could be enacted, if . . .
Without constructing model caravels
of balsa-wood or plastic, I saw skies
between the masts, inferred a different life
from never having left the skiff

moored at a dock of dark mahogany
claw-feet of overstuffed postwar club chairs
whose own piled or brocade upholstery
recalled cities that were not anywhere

inscribed in that apartment's memory.
There was only one window, opening on
an alley, garbage cans, one tree, a square
of sky on which the day's calligraphy
scribbled in slate-gray rain, anticipation
of hills, split open any horizon.

Now, even tawdry dreams turn polyglot,
suggestion of the wished-for western wind.
Two syntaxes, more tenses, alternate
merging reflections that are less than kind
(and more than kin) into a better plot
that has to do with transformation. Waking
was easy. The street outside was wet: it rained
all night. The sky's washed clean, and I am not
anticipating any leave-taking
but the rain's when it closed off the morning.

From "O Caravels"
—Guy Goffette

You never leave.
        —RIMBAUD

I

A child, I knew how sweet departure was
from having never left the skiff
of hills, split open any horizon
but the rain's when it closed off the morning

and that I'd have to find at any cost
the right light so that I could fix the seas
in their places on the map and not
overflow the lines. I was ten and

had more voyages in my pockets
than the great explorers, and if
I agreed to trade Sierra

Leone for Yakoutia, it's really
because the snowy frame of lace
around the stamp was sturdier.

Friends and Daughters

The mother, in a flannel dressing-gown,
holds her thin, flame-haired daughter on her knees,
the Shorter Version of her energies.
Here, three girls lark on the muddy lawn,
her two in shorts, despite the chill of June
in Dublin, mine in paisley jeans, a sixties
rip-off, taller, smiling, almost at ease.
Here is the mother reading at noon, alone.
Turn your eyes from the children, heated to flames
in spring-sap brandy, uprushing to be grown,
and, evanescent rainlight, they are gone
into air, liquid, fire. Turn your eyes from the friends
setting all their volatile precedents:
three snapshots, with a date on the back, their names.

Pomegranate

Mid-October, ripe as a pomegranate
on a market-stall, in a myth so often
turned by Western women, you'd think that each one
had lived the story.

He, from elsewhere, draws upon other stories,
other rhythms in which to tell them, echoes,
numbers, and an alphabet which I trace out
halting and childish,

while he speaks to the Greek, the Kurd, the Spaniard,
questions language with the displaced Iraqi
and the Jew who riddled in nomanslanguage
the trope of "homeland."

Waits, and reads the paper, in some small café:
who will be the foreigner, who, the lover?
After years' displacements, the words risk having
a double meaning—

risk, or have the luck of a double meaning
in their roots. Some words have their own ideas,
so a line with bullets in it transforms them
deftly, to sparrows.

Why not, waiting, write in the spiral notebook:
birds, remembered bullets, the rooftop terrace
pots of bougainvillea? Autumn rain clouds
mass above rooftops

in a city where women read the paper
in cafés, yes, just the way he does, waiting
for, not more than sunlight, the jolt of caffeine,
a glass of water.

I reach out and pick up the pomegranate,
palm its blemished rind, purple-pocked by clustered
egg-like ruby seeds, that could splash a bloodstain
across a doorstep,

memorizing new verbs and nouns: home, journey,
write, school, study, family, brother, sister
and a mother's name, which can mean, in context,
pilgrim, or exile.

1953: The Bus to Menton

Her own displacement seemed easy in comparison.
She had been a reporter. She would be a novelist
and her country (she'd write about it) seemed provincial.
The war was over. Near the roadside, sheaves
were tied. Gossip behind her, a new dialect. She listened.
Beyond sprawled olive-terraces, unlike the farms

of home, whose outbuildings circled like a garrison.
Her notebook's lined page waited to be kissed.
The noon heat condensed into a mortal chill
up her spine. A blondish man with rolled-up sleeves
had pushed the bus window open. Sunlight glistened
on the long number tattooed on one of his sunburned arms.

The barricades along the avenue
presage the arrival of a parade.
A holiday, a hero, of which war?

In the city fissured by war and war,
floodlights and sirens slash the avenue.
Market-stalls spill, A truck bomb, an air raid:

slow-motion now, the desperate parade
stagnates, as if blocked traffic stood for war,
as if death in the street were something new,

while new parades clear avenues for war.

Ghazal: The Beloved

Remembering Faiz Ahmed Faiz

Lines that grapple doubt, written because of the beloved:
when grief subsides, what survives the loss of the beloved?

Your every declaration is suspect.
That was, at least, the departing gloss of the beloved.

Were you merely a servant of the state
or (now you give the coin a toss) of the beloved?

How pure you were, resistant in an orchard.
Peace with justice: the cause of the beloved.

A scent of hyacinth clings to your fingers,
of sap from a broken leaf, of moss, of the beloved.

Ambiguous predators howl within earshot.
You would like to curl up between the paws of the beloved.

Now uniforms cite scripture to erase you.
Only rabble and vermin die under the laws of the Beloved.

Who signed the warrant that sealed you in this cell?
Who read your messages? Who was the boss of the beloved?

How pure you were, how abject you are now,
waterboarded after the double-cross of the beloved.

You are promised release on the recognizance
(will this be a redemptive clause?) of the beloved.

For Kateb Yacine

(Algerian playwright, novelist, poet and activist, 1929–1989)

A moment jumps the interval; the next
second, a sudden dissonance swells up,
a crack down the smooth surface of the cup,
a dialogue with mistranslated text,
a tense the narrative poises, perplexed,
upon. The dancers and the singer stop,
swirled, each, in shadow like a velvet cape,
potential, and ambiguously sexed.
A gender and a nationality
implicit in the ululation rise
from a long throat to claim or compromise
privilege; responsibility
in texture, in that wound of sound, that vexed
surface, which could detonate, could drop.

Could drop into the anonymity
of headlines: war and fear and fear of war
and war abetted by ambient fear
honed to a hunger by publicity.
But there is a room above the street, a three-
o'clock winter sun, the nuanced, near-
ly translucent voice of a counter-tenor
threading a cantata by Scarlatti.
There were the exile's words in Arabic
anathematizing any deity
if slaughter is sanctified in its name;
the voice, the struggle from which words became
corporeally transformed to music.
There is the emblematic cup of tea.

There is the emblematic pot of tea
steaming on a wooden bench between
antagonists engaged in conversation
halfway to official enmity,
halfway to some compromise they can agree
upon, and not lose face. A city drones
and screeches in the crepuscule beyond
the room, in contrapuntal energy.
They keep sentences moving, savor the way
to pluck the pertinent or flabby phrase
and skin and gut it, twisting in the air:
a game they magisterially play
like diplomats, not gray-sweatered, gray-haired
exiles filling the breach of winter days.

Exiles filling the breach of winter days
with rhetoric have nothing, but have time
for rhetoric as logical as rhyme.
Meanwhile a speechwriter drafts the ukase
which, broadcast to a military base,
sends children and their city up in flames.
Meanwhile, an editor collects our names
and texts in protest: we can only guess
who else is keeping tabs, who else will be
pilloried in an op-ed in the *Times,*
distracted by brief notoriety
or told a passport will not be renewed.
Imagined exiles, with what gratitude
I'd follow your riposted paradigms.

To make of his riposte a paradigm,
he conjured Nedjma from the wilderness
behind his distance-mined electric face.
Kahina, Nedjma, Ummi, a woman's name
ejaculated to a stadium:
a heroine, a first lover unseen
for decades, a mother who mimed, silence upon
women's silence screamed past millennium.
Another silence, the interlocutor
who argued over wine with Paul Celan
until the words were not German or French
in the cold hypothesis of the Seine,
no longer comforter, companion, tutor
to the last Jew on the November bench.

If the last Jew on the November bench
shivered, rose, walked to the rue de Tournon
and ordered a Rémy and a *ballon*
de rouge with Roth, could it blot out the stench
of ash and lies for both? (Over the ranch
in Texas what smoke rises in premoni-
tory pillar?) The gaunt Algerian
asynchronous, among them, needs to quench
an equal thirst. We all had pseudonyms,
code-names, pet-names, pen-names: *noms de guerre,*
simple transliterations, unfamiliar
diphthongs in rote order, palindromes
and puns patched on the untranslatable
(unuttered, anguished) root of a syllable.

Unuttered, anguished, roots of a syllable
in her first language threaded the page she'd sign
(written at night, in a strange town, hidden
among strangers, once betrayed) "Nicole
Sauvage."
   Sun gilds the roof of the town hall,
its bridal parties gone, too cold, too late.
The February sky is celibate,
precipitated towards a funeral.
Yes, war will come and we will demonstrate;
war will come and reams of contraband
reportage posted on the Internet
will flesh out censored stories, second-hand.
Tire-treads lumbering towards its already-fixed
moment jump the interval: this war, the next.

("Nicole Sauvage" was the pseudonym used by the writer Nathalie Sarraute during the Nazi occupation of France during World War II, in the village where she went into hiding with her daughters after being denounced as a Jew by neighbors in another village.)

Ghazal: Waiting

What follows when imagination's not inspired by waiting,
body and spirit rendered sick and tired by waiting?

Wrinkles, stock market losses, abscessed teeth, rejection
    slips:
some of the benefits acquired by waiting.

Taught from childhood that patience is a virtue,
she thought that she could get what she desired by waiting.

History, a child at the chapter's cusp
will only find out what transpired by waiting.

Does anyone escape alienated labor's
cycle of being hired, exploited, made redundant, fired, by
    waiting?

He rolls a pen like a chess-piece between thumb and
    forefinger:
he won't emerge from the morass in which he's mired by
    waiting.

If poetry's imagination's daughter,
didn't someone say that she was sired by waiting?

She raised her children, wrote at dawn, ignored the factions,
arrived at being read, remembered and admired by waiting.

Once a pair of lovers downed shots in a Chelsea bar,
their nerves and fantasies hot-wired by waiting.

Sweating, shackled and blindfolded in a basement,
will I get out, the hostage (of whom) inquired, by waiting?

Glose

And I grew up in patterned tranquility
In the cool nursery of the new century.
And the voice of man was not dear to me,
But the voice of the wind I could understand.
         —ANNA AKHMATOVA, "Willow"
      Translated by Judith Hemschemeyer

A sibilant wind presaged a latish spring.
Bare birches leaned and whispered over the gravel path.
Only the river ever left. Still, someone would bring
back a new sailor middy to wear in the photograph
of the four of us. Sit still, stop *fidgeting.*
—Like the still-leafless trees with their facility
for lyric prologue and its gossipy aftermath.
I liked to make up stories. I liked to sing:
I was encouraged to cultivate that ability.
And I grew up in patterned tranquility.

In the single room, with a greasy stain like a scar
from the gas fire's fumes, when any guest might be a threat
(and any threat was a guest—from the past or the future)
at any hour of the night, I would put the tea things out
though there were scrap-leaves of tea, but no sugar,
or a lump or two of sugar but no tea.
Two matches, a hoarded cigarette:
my day's page ashed on its bier in a bed-sitter.
No godmother had presaged such white nights to me
in the cool nursery of the young century.

The human voice distorted itself in speeches,
a rhetoric that locked locks and ticked off losses.
Our words were bare as that stand of winter birches
while poetasters sugared the party bosses'
edicts (the only sugar they could purchase)
with servile metaphor and simile.
The effects were mortal, however complex the causes.
When they beat their child beyond this thin wall, his
     screeches,
wails and pleas were the gibberish of history,
and the voice of man was not dear to me.

Men *and* women, I mean. Those high-pitched voices—
how I wanted them to shut up. They sound too much
like me. Little machines for evading choices,
little animals, selling their minds for touch.
The young widow's voice is just hers, as she memorizes
the words we read and burn, nights when we read and
burn with the words unsaid, hers and mine, as we watch
and are watched, and the river reflects what spies. Is
the winter trees' rustling a code to the winter land?
But the voice of the wind I could understand.

For Anna Akhmatova

Who had been in love with her that summer? Did it matter?
The incidental willow is what she would remember,
bare like a silver brooch on a sky of foxfur
during the winters of famine and deportations.
She wished she had something more cheerful to show them:
a list of the flowering shrubs in a city park,
lovers and toddlers asprawl behind rosebushes;
workers with mallets indulging in horseplay
while knocking partitions of sheetrock to splinters:
energy's avatars, feminine, masculine.
Forehead against the cold pane, she would always be
ten-and-a-half years older than the century.

She remembered Mother reading them Nekrasov
as they ate sardines with white cheese and tomatoes
while sun set late on the same seacoast where Tomis
had sheltered and repelled an exiled poet.
She would eat the same briny cheese in the heat of Tashkent
waiting for news from re-named Leningrad.

It had pleasured her, a language which incised
choreographed chance encounters, almost-uttered
words, eye-contact, electricity
of an evaded touch: she wrote about
brief summers, solitude's inebriation
in the dusk that fell at almost midnight.
(Louise Labé in a less clement climate,
with electricity and indoor plumbing.)
She and her friends and lovers chiselled lyrics
until the decade (what did they think of revolution?)
caught up with them, the elegant companions,
and set them to a different exercise.

(Which travelling companions would you pick?
Who would have chosen to endure Céline?
Pasternak wrote a paean to Stalin;
Donne, for Pascal, would be a heretic.)

Something held her back from choosing exile
when the exacting enterprise went rotten
Russia was not her motherland: it was St. Petersburg,
the birch-lined corridors of Tsarskoye Selo—
but she was not retained by bark-scales spreading
up her limbs, with a god's breath in her ears: there
were her threatened friends, her son in prison
(who would not understand her coded letters
or what had held her back from choosing exile
after she did the paperwork to place him
in the Russian Gymnasium in Paris
the year his father met a firing squad;
and Marina—who would not live long—
wrote, she would meet them at the train station).
Tinned fish, gas rings, staggering armchairs, stained toilets
—mass graves of compromising manuscripts.
Was her exigent Muse the despised dictator
who censored, exiled, starved, imprisoned, murdered,
hurting the prodigy of birch and willow
into her late genius of debridement?
"Submissive to you? You must be out of your mind . . ."

How could she imagine, the *"gay little sinner,"* up
daybreak to dawn, the exactions of history?
City rerouted for transit to labor camps,
first husband shot in prison, their son in prison,
then in a labor camp, on the front, then still in prison.
She, over fifty, grown aquiline, vigilant,

larger than life, *"casta diva,"* her arias
camouflaged witness, evoking the dailiness
veiled in translation or foreign geographies.
Can you, yourself, in your eyrie, imagine it
while an empire's gearshifts creak behind you?

She made her despair the Virgin's or Cleopatra's
—under the circumstances, not outrageous.
She would write in praise of peace brought by the tyrant
if her lines might evoke an adjective passed down
from underling to underling until
some hungry guard unlocked a door . . . It didn't
happen. Her son called her superficial.
Larger than life, with all her flaws apparent
she rolled on the floor and howled in indignation,
more like the peasant she had come to resemble
than Anna Comnena or Cleopatra
or the ikon of words who was asked by other women
at the prison wall *"Can you describe this?"*

Once, in a youthful funk, she had made a poem of
her son (then just four) at her churchyard graveside
unable to resurrect his flighty mother
except to the balance sheet of her defections.
She was alone, and he was alive, in prison.
The impatient butterfly of Tsarskoye Selo
a solid matron, stood below the frozen
walls, with her permitted package, like the others—
whether they had been doting or neglectful mothers.

Paragraph

Another morning opens up its hand
on loss and possibility at once.
Your face is wrinkled. The blank page is lined.
A year turned over in its furrows; months
narrowed the light, which now has widened
three weeks past solstice, lengthening beyond
the cloudbank or the elegy,
the unlucky anniversary.
The father who outlived his daughter writes
something about the snow
which covered the cow pasture in last night's
sub-zero freeze. The four-New-Year's-ago
manuscript's a book—cold as a monument, the daughter
who outlived her father thinks. Outside her study window
blackbirds preen on iridescent water.

AN OCEAN BETWEEN US

Ghazal: *kana bahrun m'a beini wa beiniki*

Was there loyalty, envy, devotion between us?
More like a dizzying pendulum's motion between us.

After the silence and the damp morning chill
a new conversation would grate like corrosion between us.

There was too little or too much to say,
not enough words, too much emotion between us.

Who'll be the first to make the indelible move,
pick up and drink down the vial of potion between us?

Orgasmic fireworks were a metaphor:
there was a different kind of explosion between us.

Must a mountain crumble before we can really speak?
Must I wait for an aeon's erosion between us?

The morning light spells its name on my white coffee cup
but it aches with absence: *there is an ocean between us.*

Lettera amorosa

Where's the "you" to whom I might write a letter?
There are dozens, none is the "thou" I never
did engage in dialogue: was I talking
to myself, loudly?

You, your lion's mane and your pale-rimmed glasses,
buccaneering over the swells of panic,
settled now, with a child, career and spouse in
lower Manhattan?

You, who picked the riverbank where we often
told our days with coffee at almost-twilight
to announce irrevocable departure?
You're gone, you said so.

You, but who are you, if I never met you,
man or woman, mother tongue French or English
(maybe Arabic), you're a word, a nameless
presence, night-fancied.

Letter, then, to light, which is open-ended,
folds, expands, but even on winter mornings
faithfully attends to the correspondence,
answers the question.

Ghazal: Myself

They say the rules are: be forgotten, or proclaim myself.
I'm reasonably tired of that game, myself.

I watched some friends rush off, called by the wild,
and stayed home to make coffee for the tame myself.

There are actions I was pressured or seduced to,
but for omissions, I can only blame myself.

Do I think that my averted glance
nullifies suffering? First of all, I maim myself.

Did sex ever seem like work to *you*?
Sometimes, five minutes after I came myself.

Although I'm manifestly "not my type"
the one in my bed this morning was, all the same, myself.

Not Elektra, Clytemnestra, nor Iphigenia,
I'll remain an unsung keeper of the flame myself.

Burnished oak surrounds a rectangle of glass
at the top of the stairs, in which I frame myself.

A signature hangs, unwritten, below the last
line on the page, where I'm obliged to name myself.

Letter to Alfred Corn

Alfred, we both know there's little dactylic pentameter
that can be spotted and quoted from classic anthologies
(although Hephaestion's *Handbook on Meters* cites "Atthis, I
loved you once long ago" as an example, without much on
Sappho, but still, could a presence be much more felicitous?)
so this epistle is, much like good friendship, unorthodox,
framed both by Sappho *and* schoolmasters, and, overseeing the
words of itinerants, Wystan? Jean-Arthur? Elizabeth?
Aimé and Léopold lighting the Left Bank with Négritude?
August has shut down the shops and cafés on my market
     street;
when they re-open, *la rentrée*, fresh start, it will be without
me. I'll be back in New York, feeling ten times more alien
than where the polyglot boulevards intersect, linking up
11e and 20e, Maghreb, punk chic, kashruth, chinoiserie.
Once one could say that Manhattan was barely America,
which—in Manhattan—was meant as an insider's
     compliment.
Now it's as flag-ridden as the Republican "heartland," where
you behave better than Ovid in exile, not whimpering,
making the best of a stint as a scholar-in-residence.
For two good weeks we were neighbors, and living our
     parallel
lives, you at liberty, sampling the fruits of the capital—
notably, joys of the eye, its museums and boulevards,
while I attempted to pilot a relay of immigrant
artisans (David and Mario, Portuguese masons and
Nicolas, Serbian, plumber, and Sokli, Tunisian,
painter, Jérôme, electrician, from Sénégal, none of whose
papers I'd swear were in order, no more than my own are, all
working unsupervised for an unscrupulous contractor,

sleazy, incompetent, straight out of some New Wave gangster
      film,
who extracts money with threats from me, lets *them* go
      weeks unpaid)
—if I was lucky and someone showed up on the work-site
      where
shelter was knocked down to gougings in plaster, precarious
walls spouting naked bouquets of distressed electricity.
That was the place I'd returned to with certainty suddenly
gone, when my life was made moot by disease, when
      companionate
passion had turned to disdain's acrimonious grievances
and I was left a late-quinquagenarian celibate
—still, when I mounted the spiral stairs slant with three
      centuries'
steps (like the furrows defining the smile of a laureate)
I was home safe in the cave that I'd made for the possible.
(Who, though, is safe, from the "shocking disease," from the
      bulldozer
wreaking revenge for the sins of the sons on their families,
or from the dynamite-bookbag in the cafeteria,
or from the tinderbox arrogant ignorance lights for us,
turgid with power, and willing to offer up holocaust?)
Ambulant scholar uprooted from tenure-track coteries
(who dared rip open the envelopes of the academy)
you are an expert at wanderings, vagaries, pilgrimage,
sometimes volitional, sometimes compelled by necessity.
Paris was part of your salad days and your apprenticeships:
Benjamin, Baudelaire, bars, Henry James, Baroque opera.
When you returned to it, changed, had it changed for you?
      Every
street I walk down with one friend, then alone, then with
      somebody

else is three streets; is a new glyph incised on a palimpsest
someone, a painter, a novelist, poet or essayist
also inflected by naming, exulting or suffering
there, what she noticed, he turned from, we commented on
        as we
strolled, in no hurry, towards something convivial.
                                        (We could have
stayed on the rue de Belleville to the Buttes-Chaumont,
        following
Breton and Aragon, seen if the statue was voluble . . .)
Late afternoon of Assumption, a holiday layered with
faces and pages and facets of (largely) this *Hexagone*:
nuns in white habits who sang a cappella, Le Thoronet's
ruins behind them sky-domed, or the nine-o'clock mass
        which was
washed in the filtered light Matisse's windows poured down
        the pews,
dramas in Vence, below, held for postprandial gossip-fests.
This year it's solo, the 3e, and who'll intercede for us
itinerants while the world goes to hell in a handbasket
(floats like a discarded dinner-dress down to the aqueduct)?
Still, the square's peaceable kingdom of Chinese and African
toddlers, mixed couples, clochards with guitar singing
        Dylan songs
—slurring the lyrics a bottle of plonk helps approximate—
stays what it's been, just as friendship seems durable. Let me at
least for your birthday, just past, be, though cautious, an
        optimist,
who loves the world both despite and because of its disarray,
planning new flâneries shared in our mutable capital.
("Atthis, I loved you then long ago when you were
a scruffy ungracious child" was my neophyte's take on it.)

Ghazal: Style

Unmistakable, that consummate style
pierces the incoherence of her late style.

One of them liked to tease out a game for hours;
the other had an eight-minute-check-and-mate style.

Count stresses; number feet: you've got the meter,
but there's no metronome to calibrate style.

Words from a dictionary; form-schemes from a textbook
provide a trot; they don't translate style.

The urban innocent, one more gay man
whose fantasy and flesh respond to straight style.

And here's another student shy of reading
the classics, for fear that they'll contaminate style.

Always clumsy performing virtue, he
accomplished wickedness with great style.

Bombast and pieties in primary colors:
"Hallmark's" the hallmark of the state style.

Events exceed what verse can render,
or even prose: you start to hate style.

If there isn't a damned thing left to say
that's not been said, mark time and cultivate style.

Letter to Hayden Carruth

Dear Hayden, I have owed you a letter for
one month, or two—your last one's misplaced. But I'm
    back in New York. The world is howling,
    bleeding and dying in banner headlines.

No hope from youthful pacifists, elderly
anarchists; no solutions from diplomats.
    Men maddened with revealed religion
    murder their neighbors with righteous fervor,

while, claiming they're "promoting democracy,"
our homespun junta exports the war machine.
    They, too, have daily prayer-meetings,
    photo-op-perfect for tame reporters.

("God Bless America" would be blasphemy
if there were a god concerned with humanity.)
    Marie is blunt about it: things were
    less awful (Stateside) in 1940.

I wasn't born . . . I've read shelves of books about
France under Vichy after the armistice:
    war at imagination's distance.
    Distance is telescoped now, shrinks daily.

Jews who learned their comportment from storm troopers
act out the nightmares that woke their grandmothers;
    Jews sit, black-clad, claim peace: their vigil's
    not on the whistle-stop pol's agenda.

"Our" loss is grave: American, sacralized.
We are dismayed that dead Palestinians,
    Kashmiris, Chechens, Guatemalans,
    also are mourned with demands for vengeance.

"Our" loss is grave, that is, till a president
in spanking-new non-combatant uniform
    mandates a war: then, men and women
    dying for oil will be needed heroes.

I'd rather live in France (or live anywhere
there's literate debate in the newspapers).
    The English language is my mother
    tongue, but it travels. Asylum, exile?

I know where I feel more like a foreigner
now that it seems my birth country silences
    dissent with fear. Of death? Of difference?
    I know which city lightens my mornings.

You had New England; I had diaspora,
an old folk song: "Wish I was where I would be,
    Then I'd be where I am not." Would that
    joy claimed its citizens, issued passports.

"First, do no harm," physicians, not presidents,
swear when inducted. I'm tired of rhetoric,
    theirs, journalists' or my own ranting.
    I'd like to hole up with Blake and Crashaw—

but there's a stack of student endeavors that
I've got to read, and write some encouraging
    words on. Five hours of class tomorrow;
    Tuesday, a dawn flight to California.

Glose

The rampart behind the leprosarium:
That also is Jerusalem.
Blue brooks cross the fields,
Light silver-leafs a stocky tree.
　　　　　　—EMMANUEL MOSES,
　　　　　　"The Year of the Dragon"
　　　　　　Translated by M. H.

Sunday noon haze on the fruit-stalls of Belleville,
a clochard's clothesline under the Pont des Arts,
the last Alsatian deli in the rue de Tourtille,
the second kosher couscous in the rue Saint-Maur.
The Northern Line at midnight back from Stockwell
via Charing Cross, since no one, not even a cab, had come.
The Black Mountains lurching past a drunken car,
a mail-van threading the Col de Vence in lunar
dawn when the town's enceinte is a columbarium.
The rampart behind the leprosarium.

An equinoctial dusk wrapping the Square
du Temple; a hangnail moon glimpsed through light rain
on the Pont Sully; the 96 bus trapped by parked
motorcycles outside the Royal Turenne,
honking, while truck fumes mount, and the bus driver
shouts at the *motards* what he thinks of them
somewhat distracting his stalled passengers
(the cyclists are pertinently not there);
the glass of water the waiter brings to him:
that also is Jerusalem.

Methods of crossing borders are diverse:
sixty years passed, and trains are innocent
again. Cream-colored cattle kneel; a lone horse
in a barnyard cocks a gray ear to the wind.
The sibilance of riverbanks, the terse
monosyllables a billboard holds
aloft above the tracks, a jet-trail's spent
calligraphy: their messages disperse
in the breached air whistling as it yields.
Blue brooks cross the fields.

In a vision of the perfected past,
a cindered path's circumference of vines
measures the play of words and breath, at last
conjoined in a few salvageable lines:
all of the hour's trajectory not lost
in burnt-out synapses of memory.
Yet some insight bestowed on aliens
inscribes the vineyard on a palimpsest
of city, valley, hills, a different city.
Light silver-leafs a stocky tree.

From "The Year of the Dragon"

—Emmanuel Moses

XLVII

The rampart behind the leprosarium:
That also is Jerusalem.
Blue brooks cross the fields,
Light silver-leafs a stocky tree.
In precious books which slip between our fingers
Each page tells a different story.
I also like to sit with you in that little café
Near the Rohin where the minutes are marked off
By the clanking of the streetcars
In February when the cold bites down
Into the porous flesh of Amsterdam's bricks
The dead rise up with the provisionally
Living and say each in turn
"How we have escaped."

Letter to Mimi Khalvati

Dear, how I hate the overblown diction of
lines for occasions: festschrifts, like elegies
    making a banal birthday seem to
    signpost a passage to unmapped wasteland,

when thoughts and smiles are fresh as they've ever been
—at least my brief years given the privilege
    of bantering across some table,
    words made more fluent by cakes or curries

or by the short time left for exchanging them:
train in an hour, espresso in Styrofoam
    cups. Ciao! I wish . . . I'll tell you next time.
    Bus to the Eurostar, airport taxi.

I'll never see the light of your memories
(joy can be shared, but losses are separate)
    though we're a lucky pair of outcasts,
    free to embellish or keep our stories.

Yours, Mimi, silver's brilliance on velvety
shapes in the no-man's-land between alphabets
    you were obliged to cross and cross to
    write in the white ink of exiled childhood.

Whose children *did* we talk about, smoking and
sipping red wine (an Indian family
    toasting some milestone near us) in the
    restaurant tucked behind Euston Station?

Two women, poised for middle-aged liberty,
still have our fledgling burdens to anchor us,
    wish they were soaring, independent,
    glad when they ground us with tea and gossip.

Think of the friendships lost to geography,
or lost to language, sex, or its absence . . . I
    send, crossing fingers, crossing water,
    bright thoughts, bright Maryam: happy birthday.

Ghazal: Nothing

You'll reap no whirlwind if you sow nothing—
hungry yourself, you'll still bestow nothing.

Market-driven to live beyond my means,
my credit's no good if I owe nothing.

Today the doctor calls with the test results.
Nothing is settled if they show nothing.

What do I answer the friend who (like time)
Can tell me nothing but "I told you so"? Nothing.

My child's gone somewhere suddenly dangerous.
I listen for some fact on the radio: nothing.

Contained within that frame of words set down
like black and white stones in a game of Go: nothing.

Reading the titles on a library shelf,
it's liberating, sometimes, to know I know nothing.

What did Louise Labé write after she turned forty?
What's left, François, of all last winter's snow? Nothing.

Thyme and cornflowers, blackberries, figs hanging over the
        wall:
late summer harvest of those who grow nothing.

What have you been doing in your room for three hours
with the door locked, blinds drawn, music blaring? Oh,
        nothing,

At the center of the paisley swirl,
the heart of the elaborate intaglio: nothing.

NAMES

From Diaspo/Renga

These renga are from a series written in alternation with the Palestinian-American poet Deema Shehabi. I have included the "prompts" from the last lines of Deema's renga that led to the ones that followed.

Five, six—and righteous,
the child in green in Gaza
stands in her wrecked home,

grubby, indignant. Her hands
point; she explains what was done

bombed, burned. "It all smells
like gas. We had to throw our clothes
away! The earrings my

father gave me!" No martyr,
resistant. The burnt cradle . . .

curtains whip across . . .

the third-floor window
in Belleville, dyed blue-purple
like the hyacinth

on the windowsill. Nedjma
does math homework. Strike today,

but school tomorrow.
Coming back from the demo
they sang in the street—

Rêve Générale!—the slogan
makes her smile. Wan winter sun . . .

Where are the hills

. . . he saw from New York . . .
"Marhaba ya Nafisa!
Girl, you watch your back!

Tanks and uniforms zap guys'
minds worse than testosterone

but you were gorgeous
reasoning as you dodged to
keep them from aiming

at the brothers behind you
dancing along the barbed wire."

. . . that your grandfather's
farm sat between, that you climbed,
a boy in summer

near the Syrian border
maybe twenty years ago?

You are still young. Our
hands touch over the open
books on the table

out of which you are teaching
your language to an old Jew.

is always

a word emerging
mid-throat, like the *ayn,* in an
emigrant winter,

a word that casts blue-white flame
across the café counter.

Nightfall. It's heady
as the red wine they're drinking
to hear each other's

stories in a third language,
the bridge on which they first met.

Her mother would say

Her mother would say
"Blacks, Puerto Ricans, Arabs . . ."
and that was enough.

The front door slammed shut on the
puzzled face of affection.

All "we" were was what
was not the darker other
with his long lashes,

with her insistent questions.
Beyond the locked door, a song.

the ocean sound in the trees,

The horse and the night
and the wide desert know me . . .
and this narrow street

where fine rain falls before dawn
and the child in the next room

coughing in her sleep,
window in November cracked
open, the Bic pen,

and the wind that slips in with
insistent chilly fingers.

* * *

The Litani flows
under the Pont Sully, past four
Arabic bookshops.

(One is run by anarchists.)
She stops to watch a barge pass.

The Crusaders gave
her those blue-green eyes. Not that
interrogative

smile at the cadence of wind
tangling her kinky black hair.

alleyway that smells of the sea

Dogs on the port street
fighting over a fish-head,
spoiled fruit—he can smell

the discarded orange peels
guards threw to exiled children.

He was sixteen then,
no dog, no child, a teacher.
Others learned to read

from the tea-stained grammar book
he'd grabbed up first when they fled.

* * *

The hallal butcher
has a charity tin for
Children of Gaza.

I pay for my leg of lamb
and drop in all of the change,

walk away up the
rue de la Roquette humming
"Guantanamera."

On the place Voltaire, a white
lady can enjoy the joke.

Sitting in a garden

Sitting on damp grass,
she recites al-Sayyab's lines
on Dickinson's lawn.

Slowly, her Anglophone friend
repeats each verse after her.

"Back in Mosul, I'll
either build a house or buy
a plot for a grave."

"*Insh'allah*, you'll build a house.
Keep that line for a poem."

For Despina

Why is it I don't like closing the curtains?
Even pinning pans of blue voile together
cuts me off too much from the winter morning's
comings and goings.

and the tall, reassuring neighbors' windows
some with window boxes, some with their shades down
some cracked open from last night, so cold air could
refresh a sleeper.

Pick the stitch up, there in the place I dropped it.
Weave the ravelled sides of the day together
if December sun in a bedroom window
calls for a garment.

There are alphabets I could still decipher,
learn to read a stanza, or write my name in.
There are conjugations of verbs instructing
speech, song and silence.

Fear or hope or both of them made of me a
child who thought I'd probably be abandoned
if I misbehaved, if I lied about my
parents—or didn't.

How are you a Jew? asked the young Greek woman
First, because I haven't the choice to not be.
Those who thought they chose found the same unchosen
barbed wire and ashes.

How am I a Jew? Through my mother's birthright,
turned into a death warrant once; excuse to
seize the farms and villages of a people
"exiled by exiles."

You, the dead, my interlocutors, whether
friends or strangers—child on a no-man's-land, her
satchel and school uniform clear in gunsights,
riddled with bullets—

while I clutch the moment, with a safe childhood
as my history, no grandparents' village,
no street where her father made shoes, his mother
measured out barley.

Strange that all I know of them is—*religion*?
Not if they had land, sent their sons to *cheder*;
Not which ones spoke Yiddish, Hungarian, or
Polish, or German.

Not which child, re-named, fed the pigs and dug up
frozen mud for potatoes; not whose notebook
browned inside a cupboard, while trains moaned through
the
Galician winter.

Must a murdered child, after generations,
be avenged by gunning down other children
far away from winter and pigs, potatoes
and nameless railroads?

"Preening left-wing Jews" mourn beside the cinder-
block debris where somebody's mother rolled up
cheese in dough while somebody's child unwisely
said, "Liberation."

If a Jew may not deconstruct the question
(two Jews, didn't we say, and three opinions?)
if they call the peacemakers anti-Semites,
who are my cousins?

Lost lands which I never would call my country . . .
How are you American? she might ask me.
Language, economic determination . . .
Once, it was lucky.

Ghazal: *dar al-harb*

I might wish, like any citizen to celebrate my country
but millions have reason to fear and hate my country.

I might wish to write, like Virginia: as a woman, I have none,
but women and men are crushed beneath its weight: my
      country.

As English is my only mother tongue,
it's in English I must excoriate my country.

The good ideas of Marx or Benjamin Franklin
don't excuse the gulags, or vindicate my country.

Who trained the interrogators, bought the bulldozers?
—the paper trails all indicate my country.

It used to be enough to cross an ocean
and view, as a bemused expatriate, my country.

The June blue sky, the river's inviting meanders:
then a letter, a headline make me contemplate my country.

Is my only choice the stupid lies of empire
or the sophistry of apartheid: my country?

Walter Benjamin died in despair of a visa
permitting him to integrate my country.

Exiles, at least, have clarity of purpose:
can say my town, my mother and my fate, my country.

There used to be a face that looked like home,
my interlocutor or my mate, my country.

Plan your resistance, friends, I'll join you in the street,
but watch your backs: don't underestimate my country.

Where will justice and peace get the forged passports
it seems they'll need to infiltrate my country?

Eggplant and peppers, shallots, garlic and cumin:
let them be, married on my plate, my country.

Names

1.

A giant poplar shades the summer square.
Breakfast shift done, Reem smooths her kinky mass
of auburn curls, walks outside, her leaf-print dress
green shadow on post-millennial bright air.
It's almost noon. I smell of sweat. I smell
despite bain-moussant and deodorant,
crumpled and aging, while recognizant
of luck, to be, today, perennial
appreciating trees. The sky is clear
as this in Gaza and Guantánamo
about which I know just enough to mourn
yesterday's dead. The elegies get worn
away, attrition crumbles them into
chasm or quicklime of a turning year.

2.

Be mindful of names. They'll etch themselves
like daily specials on the window glass
in a delible medium. They'll pass
transformed, erased, a cloud the wind dissolves
above the ruckus of the under-twelves
on the slide, the toddlers on the grass,
the ragged skinny guy taking a piss
in the bushes, a matron tanning her calves
on a bench, skirt tucked around her knees.
A sparrow lands in the japonica;
as if it were a signal, all at once
massed pigeons rush up from adjacent trees,
wingbeats intrusive and symphonic—a
near total silence is the clear response.

3.

The actress reading sonnets from "The Quest"
made Auden seem, as far as I could tell,
less than Péguy, more than Marie Noël.
The Belgian poet preened. His last, or latest
girlfriend, my neighbor, not quite at her best
in crushed green velvet and a paisley shawl
was looking at once lovely and unwell.
I had to go. I could deduce the rest,
and there was a dinner in the 10e.
I walked up the rue du Temple in the fog,
not a mist of exile and erasure,
but one from which memory and nomenclature
engage (Thank you, Wystan) in a dialogue
with dark streets redolent of almost-home.

4.

Four firelit mirrors lining the Corsican
restaurant's walls reflected divergencies—
Palestinian, Syrian, Lebanese,
Russian, expat Jewish American.
A new war had begun that afternoon;
The shrinking world shrieked its emergencies
well beyond our capabilities
if not to understand, to intervene,
though Mourad, who practices medicine,
has made of intervention a career.
Khaled spent decades studying history
in the jaws, shall we say, of an emergency.
Start another bottle of rough-tongued wine,
that sanguine glitter in the midnight mirror.

5.

Edinburgh airport seems provincial when
you're headed back to CDG/Roissy
in dusty sunlight of a mid-July
midday. I had an hour. But there was Hind
(we'd been at the same conference all weekend)
who had three connections: Heathrow, Cairo,
Beirut, where the runways had been bombed,
to Damascus. With airport Starbucks, we brainstormed
the thesis-in-progress she'll have to write
in English if she's going to publish it:
Lesbian writers from the Arab world.
Boarding call. I don't know if she got home.
I e-mailed her. I haven't heard from her.
The war had started five days earlier.

6.

Noura is writing about women also: women
and war. She sends an e-mail from Mosul:
The books arrived, and they are beautiful.
I know, of course, the work of Fadwa Touqan
but since the invasion and the occupation
it is hard to find books, even in Arabic.
Attached is the synopsis of my post-doc
proposal and the draft of a translation.
I cannot visit my old teacher in Baghdad:
because I am Sunni and from Mosul
I would be immediately slain.
Through the cracked prism of Al-Andalus
we witness, mourning what we never had.
(The war goes on and on and on and on.)

7.

A waxing moon, tailwind of a return,
but to what? Life on the telephone,
letters typed on a computer screen
which no one needs to file or hide or burn
at the storm-center of emergency
where there is no coherent narrative.
With no accounting of my hours to give
black holes gape open in my memory.
If there's some story here, it isn't mine,
but one I can imperfectly discern
from what can be imperfectly expressed
by third parties in second languages.
The shots, far off, the power cut, the line
interrupted, the fact I did not learn.

8.

The names have been changed. Nobody's sister
will be gunned down because her brother
shook hands with one politician or another
or because a well-meaning woman activist kissed her
father on both cheeks the way we do
here (thinking, we're all Mediterranean
after all). Nobody's J-1
visa will be revoked because of the conference she went to
in Caracas, or, worse, Tehran.
We have an almost-fiction with mnemonic
cues, which could be proper names, or dates.
Sipping another empire's bitter tonic
an inadvertent exile contemplates
Harvard Square's night-lights on Ramadan.

Ghazal: *min al-hobbi m'a qatal*

For Deema Shehabi

You, old friend, leave, but who releases me from the love that
    kills?
Can you tell the love that sets you free from the love that
    kills?

No mail again this morning. The retired diplomat
stifles in the day's complacency from the love that kills.

What once was home is across what once was a border
which exiles gaze at longingly from the love that kills.

The all-night dancer, the mother of four, the tired young
    doctor
all contracted HIV from the love that kills.

There is pleasure, too, in writing easy, dishonest verses.
Nothing protects your poetry from the love that kills.

The coloratura keens a triumphant swan-song
as if she sipped an elixir of glee from the love that kills.

We learn the maxim: "So fine the thread,
so sharp the necessity" from the love that kills.

The calligrapher went blind from his precision
and yet he claims he learned to see from the love that kills.

Spare me, she prays, from dreams of the town I grew up in,
from involuntary memory, from the love that kills.

Homesick soldier, do you sweat in the glare of this
    checkpoint
to guard the homesick refugee from the love that kills?

Glose

the death of a sparrow has blackened the snow
But nothing consoled her
Who is the night among all nights? she asked the owl
but the owl doesn't think, the owl knows
                    —VÉNUS KHOURY-GHATA, *from* "Nettles"
                              Translated by M. H.

Dumb heat, not snow, sheathes Paris in July
and sheathes suburban Washington.
Planes rip through the fabric of a frayed
afternoon torn open
by words no afterwards will clarify.
Knowing what happened, no one will know.
We had a friend; she had a young son.
There was exile, its weight on a day.
There was the heart's ice, its insistent glow.
The death of a sparrow has blackened the snow.

Trope upon silvered trope, of what might a mirror
remind her: copper, black silk, the eloquence
intelligence gives eyes? Reflected terror
that conscripted all intelligence.
I am a great way off and cannot come nearer.
I do not know what the night or the mirror told her
or the sense of the words she wrote when nothing made
        sense,
or if they made a sense that seemed clearer and clearer.
The child raised his arms to be lifted, to be held, to hold her,
but nothing consoled her.

Put the morning away in the murk of myth:
not the unthinkable, but Radha's dance
breaking her bangles, imploring the dark god with
metered and musical lamentations,
80

repeated measures meant to distance death
suggest a redemptive spiral for the soul
(child, child bleeding to death, no second chance)
 in the containment of despair and wrath
within the peopled descent of the ritual.
(Who is the night among all nights? she asked the owl.)

No dark god was there, and no god of light.
There are women and men, cruel or fallible.
No mild friend picked up the telephone at the right
moment; some Someone was unavailable.
The morning which paled from an uneventful night
would have been ordinary, except that she chose.
Interrogate the hours, invent some oracle
flying overhead, read fate into its flight.
We think the snow was blackened by dead sparrows,
but the owl doesn't think; the owl knows.

From "Nettles"
—Vénus Khoury-Ghata

it should have been beautiful and it was merely sad
gardens departed this life more slowly than men
we would eat our sorrow down to the last drop then
belch it in splinters in the face of the cold
the sun's spirit kept the sun from warming us
a sun that eventually ran dry   from so much
          concentration
It was elsewhere
it was a very long time ago
tired of calling us the mother left the earth to enter the earth
seen from above she looked like a pebble
seen from below she looked like a flaking pinecone
sometimes she wept   in sobs that made the foliage
          tremble
life, we cried out to her, is a straight line of noises
death an empty circle
outside there is winter
the death of a sparrow has blackened the snow
But   nothing consoled her
Who is the night among all nights? she asked the owl
but the owl doesn't think, the owl knows

BLASONS

BLASONS

Ghazal: Disease

That man succumbing slowly to a known disease
prefers fictional plagues to his (banal and fatal) own disease.

A vague malaise, an ache, an itch, then bloody flux
and fevers: diagnosis of full-blown disease.

Why does the prisoner hobble toward the tribunal?
Not *our* doing: afflicted since childhood with a bone disease!

Imported violence? as if we hadn't provided
fertile environment for home-grown disease.

Salads and music and five-story walk-ups:
hopeful precautions taken to postpone disease.

As an alternative to nonexistence,
old age is welcome respite, not a crone disease.

For two years the scholar put aside her books and papers
and wallowed in "I can't bear to be alone" disease.

Settlers and missionaries were canny farmers
reaping an empire where they'd sown disease.

Not Blake's renascent lamb, Dolly's cold mutton:
when we clone life, it seems we clone disease.

Distracted, the midwife washes a healthy baby;
her eyes brighten with focus when she's shown disease.

Here is Medusa staring in the mirror,
scrying her face for symptoms of the stone disease.

Glose

Blood's risks, its hollows, its flames
Exchanged for the pull of that song
Bone-colored road, bone-colored sky
Through the white days of the storm.
    —CLAIRE MALROUX, "Storm"
            translated by M. H.

Once out of the grip of desire,
or, if you prefer, its embrace,
free to do nothing more than admire
the sculptural planes of a face
(are you gay, straight or bi, are you *queer*?)
you still tell your old chaplet of names
which were numinous once, you replace
them with adjectives: witty, severe,
trilingual; abstracting blood's claims,
blood's risks, its hollows, its flames.

No craving, no yearning, no doubt,
no repulsion that follows release,
no presence you can't do without,
no absence an hour can't erase:
the conviction no reason could rout
of being essentially wrong
is dispelled. What feels oddly like peace
now fills space you had blathered about
where the nights were too short or too long,
exhanged for the pull of that song.

But peace requires more than one creature
released from the habit of craving
on a planet that's mortgaged its future
to the lot who are plotting and raving.

There are rifts which no surgeon can suture
overhead, in the street, undersea.
The bleak plain from which you are waving,
mapped by no wise, benevolent teacher
is not a delight to the eye:
bone-colored road, bone-colored sky.

You know that the weather has changed,
yet do not know what to expect,
with relevant figures expunged
and predictions at best incorrect.
Who knows on what line you'll be ranged
and who, in what cause, you will harm?
What cabal or junta or sect
has doctored the headlines, arranged
for perpetual cries of alarm
through the white days of the storm?

Storm
—Claire Malroux

Through the white days of the storm
Bone-colored road, bone-colored sky
High vessels, swaying in place
With flanks open wide to the foe
The perfidious Piper—the same
One who drew young leaves out with his flute
From their seeping, motherly jail
In his wake, flowers and fruits,
Blackbirds, canticles, prophecies
Duets and duels of the sun and moon
The snow's caress, fur of forgetfulness
And the children circling the masts
Plunging entranced toward the routs
Blood's risks, its hollows, its flames
Exchanged for the pull of that song
Bone-colored road, bone-colored sky
Through the white days of the storm.

Blasons

I woke up in the middle of the night
because there was a noise. I vaguely heard
rustling, as if pages were being turned.
In the half-darkness (light was filtering in
from streetlamps affixed to the façade
of the building across the street) I saw
a book as massive as a cinder-block
on my desk. It was open to a page
where, even from my pillow, I could see
ciphers within illuminated scrolls.

Ciphers within illuminated scrolls
of paisley on the summer draperies
drawn on a dormant window facing mine
were, in the penumbra, visible.
You could open the window, said a voice
which might have been a child's, except I knew
it was my sister's, distorting my own,
a mirror facing a grimacing child.
The streetlamp caught, irrelevant detail
a scimitar of scar across her chest.

A scimitar of scar across her chest
identified the outbound voyager
(if only for the annals of the scar)
waiting for the southbound five-o'clock train.
It was Pentecost and the trains ran late.
A pyramid of canvas suitcases
was guarded by a brindled mongrel with
the white harness of a seeing-eye dog.
Had the blind man gone for cigarettes?
Dog, woman, man, someone is in disguise.

Dog, woman, man, someone is in disguise
masked in a carnival of departure.
Winged and illuminated from within,
the season hangs heavy from the branches.
A crowd gathered on the station platform
around the suitcases. Unguarded bags
have not contained manuscripts or foundlings
since Oscar Wilde was sent to Reading Gaol.
The woman in dark glasses asked herself
if every shrouded object were suspect.

If every shrouded object were suspect
the tower sheeted for a year in white
waxed sailcloth would menace the avenue.
The martyr's flop of bodies between sheets
does after all suggest that "little death"
but to whom exactly, who might have felt
ungratified after orgasm, regret
that a small fizzle of the nerves was not
epiphany. Elusiveness provokes
suspicion of the hooded clitoris.

Suspicion of the hooded clitoris
which has no conscience but which rarely lies
suggests implies remembers this or that:
her skirt spread out, astride his thighs surprised
into multiple climaxes. Eighteen,
the girl is not in love, the girl is in
a fable about curiosity.
The moral of the fable has perhaps
to do with what keys into memory:
prime numbers, rhymes, gunpowder synapses.

Prime numbers, rhymes, gunpowder synapses,
genera and species of herbaceous
plants, case endings of Greek nouns, breeds of
working dogs, three psalms in two languages
constitute the mnemonic furniture,
redemptive pastimes, of the desperate
or the recidivist insomniac.
The traveler whose train is late recites
multiplication tables to delay
not coming, but going unwelcomed home.

Not coming but going unwelcomed home
from somewhere imagination was piqued
to somewhere that would flatten it, tense on
the quai, extended like a leitmotif,
the sister of the writer, in her dark
glasses and a cap which covered her shaved
head (bared, out of place as an open fly),
remarked that waiting attenuates time
and the boredom which precedes the train gave
an illusion of immortality.

An illusion of immortality
in gestures which become quotidian:
being in the same place at the same time
daily, or once a season, once a year.
A haircut in the second week of May;
in December, the pelvic sonogram.
Twenty-six years ago, her mother died.
At ten in the morning at the café
the waitress with the ponytail arrives
for the lunch service and the afternoon.

For the lunch service and the afternoon
coffee to be served, there must be water,
cups, tables upright, only traffic noise,
the adrenaline of recollection.
The train pulls to the platform in sunlight;
the woman in the cap, dark glasses, black
shirt, shoulders her bag and climbs aboard
as do others. At the station café
arrivals and departures are discussed.
And was it called Spring Wind? Or Summer Rain?

And is it called Spring Wind, or Summer Rain
when sonic booms shatter kitchen windows
and present tense subverts a narrative's
deliberately aleatoric
motion? A row of vintage buses parked
near the entrance to the covered market;
police in short-sleeved summer uniforms
divert traffic. Someone is making a film.
Here and Then are remembered Here and Now
while a veil dissimulates Now and There.

While a veil dissimulates Now and There
as if it were a woman's censored face
here, the quotidian opens its eyes
on the disorder of the room it turned
from at midnight, face to a cool pillow.
Another boring day in paradise
disintegrating into a heat wave
beneath an imperturbable blue sky.
Nothing was confirmed but a question when
I woke up in the middle of the night.

Le Sancerre: September

September morning schemes of the possible:
the open sky, the late japonica, the blue day.
Noon approaches on the interplay
of what's imagined, what's forgotten, will
stay in the focus of a gaze that's still
fixed forward. There's an afterwards, to say
the rest, to mingle meanings. Let me stay
where I am, on the arc, in the break of the interval.
It rained enough through August that the trees
in the square touch a green cusp of clarity;
there's still tousled lavender near the duck pond.
The stout proprietor of the café
puts tables out for lunch on the bare ground
—the beach beneath the torn-up paving stones.

The beach beneath the torn-up paving stones
presents itself as facile metaphor:
desire beneath betrayal's scab. Not scar
yet, not yet completely overgrown
with some kind of impenetrable skin
rebarbative in aspect, not made for
caresses, nerveless. This is something tempor-
ary; what's underneath will, in its own
time emerge: abrasive, maybe, smooth
perhaps, responsive to the touch, who knows?
Noon's apex is invaded by shadows
daily more swift. Time is the truth,
it seems, untruthfully, as a cycle glows
into its decline, as the shadow grows.

Recline into the shadow as it grows
velvety like a cheek some finger yearned
to stroke. Almost everyone has returned
from shore or mountain Elsewheres. Traffic slows
around striped barriers. Jackhammer-blows
presage new trees among the paving stones.
We fiddle while some Elsewhere city burned,
to be reported on the evening news.
The *patron* tells an old man at the bar
about the night he heard Sidney Bechet.
(*A teenager dragged another boy away
from the loud conflagration in the square.
The sky spit fire.*) He changes the CD,
adjusts the volume: "Brother John's Blues."

The volume's up (*his brother . . .*) and the blues'
—Ben Webster, I coincidentally know,
being American—suave bravado
laps at the room. I'd like to write *soyeuse.*
I'd like to think that I was free to choose
my part in that identity. Below
the sax, words, clatter. (*Half an hour ago
a child was silenced, with a palm-sized bruise
across her forehead.*) I'm an American,
complicit in what I reject, deplore,
despite every petition, demonstration.
I tease out metaphors to link desire
and stasis, coffee, shadows, lavender;
in my name, sons and sisters die Elsewhere.

In my name, sons and sisters die elsewhere . . .
Words, too, are suave; but shred the silken shroud
of language and what's left? My book, the loud
conviviality across the bar,
the waitress' *"Comme d'hab?"* for my coffee are
the raw material of lies that led
to numbers in the news, to thousands dead,
to their abstraction of an endless war.
This is an autumn fantasy of peace,
abetted by a shift in languages
and light, descending and vulnerable:
the Portuguese waitress who knows my face,
the local and innocuous town hall
(whose site was the death cell of Louis Seize).

Who'll cite, who'll sell the death of whom? He says
three hundred dead this week (the radio).
Across the street, an LCD billboard
flashes a plea to free the hostages.
These blue and amber beads, these autumn days
click with their crystal conscience on a cord,
wished for, fingered for auguries, they're now
the passing present. Contrapuntal rays
of light and shadow, contrapuntal noises
call and respond. At sunset, will I sigh
in resignation, *Now my day is done*
but not the work incumbent on my day?
reminded by the chime of every line
that life is a machine for making choices.

A life is a machine for making choices
until, unscheduled, gears grind to a halt . . .
Grief thrown over a shoulder, pinch of salt,
grief that refines is not grief that destroys, is
not grief that silences the local voices
about their business on this market street.
Laundry will be done. People will eat
at the expected hour. Small children's bruises
are schoolyard rough-and-tumble superficial.
I scratch these words. Above the square, the sun
rolls half behind a storm cloud at its zenith.
These are the moments I can reckon with
whose noise and voice and choice proceed upon
September morning schemes of the possible.

Paragraphs for Hayden

1.

I'd want to talk to you about desire,
Hayden, the letter I could have written
on a subject you'd never tire
of turning in a glass, smitten
by a song, an argument, long sorrel hair,
profile of a glazed clay icon in the river,
while your knees needled and breathing
hurt, two packs a day bequeathing
what didn't, in fact, kill you in the end.
Was it a distraction
from the inexorable fear, my friend,
its five A.M. gut-contraction?
But who, of your critics or cortège, pretends
that expense of spirit, lust in action,
didn't earn you magnificent dividends?

2.

The week they told me my genetic code
was flawed, I ricocheted, desire and fear
like sun and clouds, a mood-
swing reason had no reason for
(but reason's calibrated in the blood).
Terror. Tumescence. Cloudbursts. Solitude.
No diagnosis, no beloved: balance . . .
I write, not to you, to silence.
By anybody's reckoning, now I'm "old,"
and you, an occasion instead
of an interlocutor. Aura of beaten gold
in a winter of cast lead.
Will the scale tip to the side of pleasure
when a taut cord plucked across the grid
invites, vibrates according to your measure?

3.

A taut-tuned string asserts: the girl in green,
a six-year-old in an oversized sweatshirt
in Gaza City, on a computer-screen
video, not dead, not hurt
but furious. *This is what they've done
to our house! Our clothes smell of gas! I never wore the sun-
glasses my father gave me
or the earrings my grandmother gave me!*
She tosses dark curls, speaks, a pasionaria
in front of a charred wall.
Arching her brows, she orchestrates her aria
with swift hands that rise and fall
while she forgets about fear
even as she ransacks the empty cradle
of its burnt blankets. That baby's—where?

4.

Not like "upstate," our January freeze
still killed my window-box geraniums.
Beyond that ragged khaki frieze
of dead plants, Sunday hums
up to my windows. I count each of these
hours, respite, respite, from broken treaties
uprooted orchards, shattered concrete.
Eight years later, still on the street
eight years older, two women squabble
and survive improbably.
A dark-haired boy, pale, imperturbable
sits in front of Monoprix,
wrapped in blankets, stroking a silvery cat.
Your voice begins to slip away from me.
Life is like that. Death is like that.

5.

A glass of red wine spills on the grammar book—
the pupil and the teacher gasp, then laugh.
Their voices branch into the baroque
logic of the paragraph.
Does the Brouilly birthmark presage luck
in learning elementary Arabic?
This classroom desk is a kitchen table,
but the street outside is peaceful.
Schoolchildren with satchels weave among
shoppers, construction workers, dogs.
No one here is speaking their mother tongue:
perhaps several dialogues
are contradicting contrapuntally.
Two girls in hijab with computer bags
go hand in hand into the library.

Ghazal: Begin

The energy is mounting, something will, again, begin.
You will yourself to, know you will—but when—begin.

Remember anger. Remember indignation. Remember desire.
Feel that deceptive surge of adrenaline begin.

Select a rhyme, trust syntax for reason,
let rash conjunctions of the page and pen begin.

After the last postcard, last phone call from home,
messages from somewhere beyond your ken begin.

Mathilde was eighteen. Arthur was seventeen.
One could see trouble in the ménage Verlaine begin.

Most of us first swooned in a woman's arms.
Where does that thralldom binding some to men begin?

Nights of champagne/cocaine pale into dawn.
Mornings of mint tea and ibuprofen begin.

The doctor waking in a refugee camp
heard the keened lesssons of the gaunt children begin.

Lock Bush and Cheney up with Milosevic,
then let the trial of Saddam Hussein begin.

My brave friend's gone; our leaders are blindered bastards:
Thus might an evening's reading of Montaigne begin.

As I poured that glass of wine, I thought of her
and felt the needlings of this damned migraine begin.

On the list I'm writing down of my addictions,
I'll let the oldest one, to oxygen, begin.

There where the fox was too hungry, baffled, tired,
the tracks that led the hunters to his den begin.

Perhaps it will happen if you close your eyes
and count—but very slowly—backwards from ten. Begin.

Sháhid, if my name were Witness, I would sign it.
I leave when the tired jokes about "Marilyn" begin.

A Braid of Garlic

Aging women mourn while they go to market,
buy fish, figs, tomatoes, enough *today* to
feed the wolf asleep underneath the table
who wakes from what dream?

What but loss comes round with the changing season?
He is dead whom, daring, I called a brother
with that leftover life perched on his shoulder
cawing departure.

He made one last roll of the dice. He met his
last, best interlocutor days before he
lay down for the surgery that might/might not
extend the gamble.

What they said belongs to them. Now a son writes
elegies, though he has a living father.
One loves sage tea, one gave the world the scent of
his mother's coffee.

Light has shrunk back to what it was in April,
incrementally will shrink back to winter.
I can't call my peregrinations "exile,"
but count the mornings.

In a basket hung from the wall, its handle
festooned with cloth flowers from chocolate boxes,
mottled purple shallots, and looped beside it,
a braid of garlic.

I remember, ten days after a birthday
(counterpoint and candlelight in the wine-glass),
how the woman radiologist's fingers
probed, not caressing.

So, reprise (what wasn't called a "recurrence")
of a fifteen-years-ago rite of passage:
I arrived, encumbered with excess baggage,
scarred, on the threshold.

Through the mild winter sun in February,
two or three times weekly to Gobelins, the
geriatric hospital where my friend was
getting her nerve back.

At the end of elegant proofs and lyric,
incoherent furious trolls in diapers.
Fragile and ephemeral as all beauty:
the human spirit—

while the former journalist watched, took notes and
shocked, regaled her visitors with dispatches
from the war zone in which she was embedded,
biding her time there.

Now in our own leftover lives, we toast our
memories and continence. I have scars where
breasts were, her gnarled fingers, these days, can hardly
hold the pen steady.

Thousands mourn him, while in the hush and hum of
life-support for multiple organ failure,
utter solitude, poise of scarlet wings that
flutter, and vanish.